MW01280209

Christmas Programs for Children

compiled by

Pat Fittro

STANDARD
PUBLISHING
Cincinnati, Ohio

Permission is granted to reproduce these programs for ministry purposes only—not for resale.

The Standard Publishing Company, Cincinnati, Ohio
A division of Standex International Corporation
© 1997 by The Standard Publishing Company
All rights reserved
Printed in the United States of America

ISBN 0-7847-0693-X

Contents

Dear Little Baby

Cora M. Owen

Dear little baby Jesus,
  Was laid upon the hay,
In lowly humble manger,
  On that first Christmas Day.

It's So Special

Helen Kitchell Evans

I volunteered for this program
Because it's so special for me;
It's the day our Savior was born
So this day is real special for me.

Special Gift

Alyce Pickett

I love the Lord who sent His Son
  To earth our king to be.
I love Jesus who left His home
  To come for you and me.

To Honor a King

Dolores Steger

From so very far,
They followed a star,
Their presents to bring
To honor a king.

Full of Wishes

Helen Kitchell Evans

Sometimes folks like me
Haven't much to say;
Well—I'm a little one
Who is built a different way.
I'm just full of wishes
For a merry Christmas Day.
(Clasp hand in circle from front of chest, then extend hands to audience on last line.)

Glad to Tell

Cora M. Owen

I'm glad to tell it.
Christ Jesus came,
A babe in manger.
Oh, praise His name!
That's why it's Christmas,
Because He brought
Way of salvation.
What grace was wrought!

Courage

Dixie Phillips

It takes a lot of courage to stand
  up here and say,
Christmas verses we've memorized
  and practiced night and day!
You've got to have nerves of steel
  and be able to face your fears,
I'm so glad Christmas programs
  only come once a year!

God's Gift

Orpha Thomas

We have Christmas wreaths in our
   windows,
   And lights on our Christmas tree,
I have gifts for my dad and mother,
   And they both have gifts for me.

The greatest gift this Christmastime
   Is a very special one,
It's God's gift sent from Heaven
   The gift of His only Son.

The List

Margaret Primrose

Would you like to read the list I
   wrote
   Of what I'd like to see
On Christmas morn when I wake up
   And look beneath the tree?

A computer is at the top of the list,
   Then a doll with long black hair,
A closet full of pretty clothes,
   And a box of chocolates to share.

But I know a girl could have all this
   And not be satisfied,
So this is what I'll do with my list,
   (Tears it up.)
   And thank God for what's inside.
   (Points to heart.)

For the Christ Child came to bring
   us peace
   And promised us great joy.
What greater gift could Jesus bring
   To any girl or boy?

Candles of Light

Dolores Steger

Candles of light are shining,
Shining for all to know,
Just like bright stars in the night
   sky,
Casting their eternal glow.
Jesus the Lord is now with us;
He's born on this wondrous night;
The candles grow dim in His
   presence,
For He is the world's constant light.

Glad Tidings

Alyce Pickett

Shepherds on Bethlehem's hillside
   Saw angels . . . heard them sing
Praises to God as they
      announced:
   "Good news we came to bring."

"Peace on the earth, good will to
   all,"
   Angels echoed God's word.
"For unto you is born this day
   A Savior, Christ the Lord."

The shepherds heard the glad
   tidings
   About the Christ Child's birth.
Let's listen now and hear again
   God's message sent to earth.

Rejoice and praise as those of old
   Who saw the angels bright.
Welcome again Jesus, the Lord
   Into each heart tonight.

We Jubilantly

Nell Ford Hann

We jubilantly rejoice
This month of December,
Behold! To us . . . the Prince of
    Peace . . .
    Came to earth—remember?

We joyously proclaim Him,
As voices lift in praise;
Glory to God in the highest,
    And the merriest of Christmas
    days!

A Miracle Is Coming

Dolores Steger

A miracle is coming;
I know it's on the way;
Our Christmas tree, with lights and
    bulbs,
Was put up yesterday.

And, now, we're wrapping
    presents
And writing cards to send
Real soon to all our relatives,
To each and every friend.

Myself, I wrote to Santa
And made a picture for
My mom and dad and, then, I hung
A wreath upon my door.

A miracle is coming;
I can't wait till it's here:
The miracle of Jesus' birth
We celebrate each year.

Birthday Wish

Alyce Pickett

I know why we have Christmas—
    Jesus was born that day.
I know how to talk to Him.
    He listens when I pray.
~~Tonight~~ _Today_ there's something special
    I really want to say:
It's this, "I love You, Jesus—
    Happy, happy birthday!"

Security Blanket

Margaret Primrose

First Child: *(carries a blanket)*
Why did you put your doll
On the floor in a box of hay?
Why don't you pick her up
And find some place to play?

Second Child:
Sh! This is baby Jesus
Who has no place to stay
Except with cows and sheep
Who think He's in the way.

The stable's full of dust
That makes me say, "Kerchoo!"
But Jesus doesn't cry
When it's dark and chilly, too.

First Child: *(touching the doll)*
It feels like baby Jesus
Is as cold as He can be.
Let's wrap Him in the blanket
That always goes with me.

6

Jesus' Humble Birth

Lillian Robbins

The journey was long when the
    travelers came
  From Nazareth to Bethlehem.
Men and women from all around,
  Seeking room in a local inn.

Joseph inquired of the keeper that
    night
  For a place for Mary to rest.
The response came quickly, "No
    room here,
  But this I will suggest.

There's a stable there just over the
    way.
  I'm sure the animals won't mind.
Not what you want, of that I'm sure,
  But it is a room of a kind."

Joseph led the donkey carrying
    Mary along,
  It may be a long, weary night.
But here in a stall with animals
    around,
  They could rest out of others'
    sight.

Mary with Joseph and the care of
    the Lord,
  And the holy birth was done.
A child of woman and the holy
    God,
  His only begotten Son.

Jesus was born in a humble way,
  Not royally as that of a king.
But Jesus' coming was for people
    on earth
  Salvation for all to bring.

The Holiday Place

Dolores Steger

It's not in a park;
It's not in a mall,
But, rather, in a stable's stall:
The Holiday Place.

It's not in a store;
It's not in a mart,
But, rather, in a faithful heart:
The Holiday Place.

It's in His love;
It's in His plan,
Available to every man:
The Holiday Place.

Santa! Santa!

Dolores Steger

Santa! Santa!
  What gifts have you brought?
    They're broken now
    And so, somehow,
  They're not exactly what I'd
    sought!

Father! Father!
  What gifts You have brought!
    The Babe, the Son,
    The Three in One,
  On which my heart's forever
    caught!

Jesus Is Near

(pair up — needed to fit those coming) [handwritten]

Lillian Robbins

First Child
(child 1) [handwritten]
(baby props) [handwritten]
I love the baby Jesus. *child 1*
He was born in Bethlehem. *child 2*

Fourth Child
⑦
His birthday is Christmas,
And He's God's only son. ⑧

Second Child
(hay props) [handwritten]
He was born in a stable. ③
No room was in the inn. ④

Fifth Child
(smiley face) [handwritten]
Jesus can make us happy ⑨
And take away all fear. ⑩

Third Child
(gift props) [handwritten]
There's a birthday for us to ⑤
    celebrate,
And Jesus is the one. ⑥

(star props) [handwritten]

Sixth Child
(heart props) [handwritten]
He loves every one of us, ⑪
And He is always near. ⑫

All Together
⑳ *(all)* [handwritten]
Have a happy Christmas!

(props used? → baby Jesus etc.) one child holds as say part and passes to second child in same section) [handwritten]

M-A-N-G-E-R

Dixie Phillips

(Six children line up in front of congregation, each holding a different letter to spell MANGER.)

M—is for **MANGER**, where animals are fed.
    That's what baby Jesus had for a bed.
A—is for **ANIMALS**, that were there that holy night.
    They must have thought, "What an unusual sight!"
N—is for **NOEL**, the first Christmas ever.
    Will we ever forget it? Never! Never! Never!
G—is for **GABRIEL**, an angel who came to earth,
    To tell Mary and Joseph of Jesus' soon birth.
E—is for **EVERYONE**, that includes you and me.
    Jesus came from Heaven to set us free.
R—is for **REJOICE** that's what we've come tonight to do.
    Now we have a song we'd like to sing for you. *(Point.)*
All Children: "Away in a Manger"

Say [handwritten]
Poem [handwritten]

8

Teacher reads while children act out — say underline words

Christmas Action Rhymes

Dixie Phillips

Our arms are the manger *(Fold arms to form manger.)* holding the new-
  born King.
Our hearts *(Place hands over heart.)* are His throne room, His praises
  we sing.
With love *(Cross arms over chest.)* to our Savior on this Christmas Day.
We just want to celebrate by saying, *(Cup hands around mouth.)* "Happy
  Birthday!" *children say*

Tiny baby Jesus sleeping on a bed of hay. *(Fold arms to form manger.)*
Shepherds *(Crook arm.)* walked and walked *(Walk in place.)* to see Him
  that day.
Mary rocked *(Rock arms.)* the baby all through the night.
Wise men were guided by the bright glittering light. *(Hands over head,
  wiggle fingers.)*

Where's *(Put hands over eyes & squint.)* the tiny baby born on
  Christmas Day?
What—He's sound asleep *(Face on hands.)* lying on the hay. *(Fold arms
  like manger.)*
Angels *(Flap arms.)* sing His praises to shepherds *(Crook arm.)* on
  earth.
Shepherds *(Raise arms.)* rejoice the day of His birth. *(Cradle arms.)*

Angels *(Flap arms.)* told of His coming; they sang of His birth. *(Cradle
  arms.)*
We *(Point to each other.)* are so glad that He came to earth. *(Point up,
  then down.)*
All that He *(Point up.)* wants is a place in our hearts. *(Hand on chest.)*
This Christmas, we give Him *(Point up.)* a place from the start.

9

Why We Sing Christmas Carols

Judy Carlsen

This program is designed for the smaller church, allowing all children, preschool through sixth grade, to participate. There are only a few props needed. Special costumes are optional.

Characters

Teacher	Woman
Six Children	Housekeeper
Martin Luther	Young Man
Hans	Young Woman
Katie	Phillips Brooks
Elizabeth	Man
Narrator	Child
Joseph Mohr	Redner
Franz Gruber	

Props: Six large pieces of paper or cardboard with one letter on each to spell "CAROLS"

(All children come into auditorium and sit in front pews. Beginners come up on stage.)

All: Welcome to our program!

(Six children stand in order, holding letter cards spelling C-A-R-O-L-S.)

C: C is for **Christmas** when Jesus was born.
A: A is for **angels** from Heaven adore.
R: R is for **rough**, the stable that night.
O: O is for **oxen**, with eyes shining bright.
L: L is for **love**, Jesus' love for each one.
S: S is for **songs** we sing. Praise God's Son!

Teacher: Please stand and sing "Joy to the World" with us.

(Congregation stands and sings as Beginners return to their seats. After song, everyone is seated again.)

(Four children of junior age are seated in the front row of the pews.)

#1: Teacher! Why do we have to sing these same old songs every year? What's so special about them?

Teacher: That's an interesting question! Does anyone have any ideas about why we do?

#2: It's a Christmas tradition, I guess. Right?

Teacher: Right. Any other ideas?

#3: Well, they tell about Jesus' birth.

Teacher: Good.

#4: And I like singing them. They get me in the Christmas mood.

Teacher: That's a good point too.

#1: But, where did these old songs come from?

Teacher: That is what we are going to find out right now.

"Away in a Manger"

Martin Luther

Act 1—Christmas Eve at Home

Table and three chairs set the scene. Other props needed are Bible, doll in blanket, paper, and pencil.

Martin Luther *(Humming to himself as he goes up on stage, carrying a Bible. Opens Bible to Luke 2.)* : Let's see. Ah, yes! Here it is. Children! Katie, my dear wife, it is time to read our beloved Christmas story.

(His wife, carrying "baby," and two children come on stage and sit down on the chairs. Luther stands sideways to read to them, so audience can hear him.)

Hans: Where is it found in the Bible, Papa?

Luther: Tonight we will read from Luke 2. "Joseph also went up from the town of Nazareth in Galilee to Judea, to Bethlehem the town of David, because he belonged to the house and line of David. He went there to register with Mary, who was pledged to be married to him and was expecting a child."

Elizabeth: Just like Mama was. Right, Papa? And now we have little Magdalena.

Katie: Yes, little Magdalena is our early Christmas present.

Luther: Ahem, that's right. Let's see. Oh, yes! "While they were there, the time came for the baby to be born, and she gave birth to her first-born, a son. She wrapped him in cloths and placed him in a manger, because there was no room for them in the inn."

Katie: It always makes me feel sad to hear there was no room for the baby Jesus.

Luther: I feel the same way! *(He pauses for a moment, then he closes the Bible.)* Well, children, are you ready to go to church for the Christmas Eve service? Mama will stay home with our baby, since the walk is too long and too cold for one so young.

Act 2—Following the Service

Action can take place off to one side of the platform or even near front of auditorium or in an aisle.

Luther *(looks up)*: Look, children, aren't the stars bright tonight?

Hans: They sure are, Papa! They make the snow all shiny too.

Elizabeth: I like the way the snow crunches under our feet.

Luther: Sometimes, I think of the stars as God's angels looking down and watching us.

Hans: That makes me feel good, Papa.

Elizabeth: Me too.

(They walk along in silence for a bit.)

Luther: Well, here we are at home again!

Act 3—Early Christmas Morning

Same setting as Act 1.

Luther *(yawns and stretches as he stands up at the table):* Hmm, I just can't get those words out of my mind. "No crib for a bed . . ." *(He sits down at the table and pretends to write.)* "The stars in the sky look down where He lay . . ." *(He continues writing for a bit.)*

(Katie enters.)

Katie: Martin, why are you up so early? What are you doing?

Luther: Katie, please hum for me that lullaby you always sing to the children.

(Katie begins to hum and after a few notes, he joins in.)

Luther: Yes, that is exactly it! Katie, you won't believe it, but God has given me new words for that lullaby.

Katie: I believe it, Martin. After all you have always loved to sing. Some day, maybe God will give you other songs to write down to honor Him.

Narrator *(off to the side or completely hidden from view):* Martin Luther wrote his carol way back in the early 1500s. "Away in a Manger" has become one of the best-loved Christmas carols ever written. Younger children are especially drawn to it, because of its simple words and motions to tell the story of baby Jesus' birth.

(Beginners through second grade come up on stage as piano softly plays "Away in a Manger.")

Song: "Away in a Manger" *(3 verses with motions)*

"Silent Night"

Joseph Mohr

Can be set up with two "houses" on stage by having Mohr's house with chair on one side and Gruber's house on other side of stage, with chair and table. The two houses can be further identified by simple signs with their names on them. Other props include Bible, doll, manger, paper, pencil, guitar and bell.

Act 1—Christmas Eve Call

Joseph Mohr goes on stage and sits down and reads his Bible. Suddenly, there are sharp knocks on the door. He gets up and answers it.

Woman: Oh, Pastor Mohr! I'm so glad you are home!

Mohr: Please sit down, ma'am. You look exhausted!

Woman: No, that's all right. I came down the mountain to tell you about a young couple having a baby tonight. They would dearly love to have you come and bless their house and their new child. *(As soon as she says this, she falls to the floor, completely exhausted.)*

Mohr: Oh, dear! I'd better get the housekeeper in here to help me with this lady.

(Housekeeper enters room.)

Housekeeper: Did I hear someone at the door, Pastor? *(She sees the woman on the floor.)* Hmm, I guess I did!

Mohr: Please help me get her to the chair. *(They carefully set her down on the chair.)* When she wakes up, please get her some tea and bread before she goes on her way. I'm off to see a new baby up on the mountain!

Act 2—A Newborn Child

Mohr walks and climbs for a long time, sometimes stopping to look up into the sky and breathing deep breaths of cold air.

Mohr: The stars tonight remind me of the night our Savior was born. "There were shepherds living out in the fields nearby, keeping watch over their flocks at night. An angel of the Lord appeared to them, and the glory of the Lord shone round about them, and they were terrified. But the angel said to them, 'Do not be afraid. I bring you good news of great joy that will be for all the people. Today in the town of David a Savior has been born to you; he is Christ the Lord.'"
(He comes to the door of the house and knocks a few times.)
Young Man: Ah, Pastor Mohr! How wonderful of you to come!
Mohr: Is the baby born yet? Is it a boy or a girl?
Young Man: Come and see my newborn son, Pastor.
Young Woman *(softly)*: Thank you for coming, Pastor. *(She carefully lifts her baby out of a small manger.)*
Mohr: You have a manger for your son's cradle?
Young Man: We thought it seemed right, having a baby on Christmas and all. I made it myself.
Mohr *(carefully takes the baby in his arms)*: Oh, dear God! You have blessed this loving family with a wonderful son on this holy night! What a wonderful gift you have sent from above. Thank you for this little life, which reminds us so much of your own Son, our Savior, Jesus Christ. Bless this little boy and this whole household. Amen. *(He returns the baby to his mother.)*
Young Woman: Thank you!
Young Man *(shaking Mohr's hand):* This means so much to us!
Mohr: I wouldn't have missed it for anything! Good night! *(He leaves and begins walking home, smiling and humming. As soon as he returns home, he sits down and begins writing down some thoughts on paper.)*

Act 3—Music by Franz Gruber

Mohr knocks on door of Gruber's house.

Gruber: Pastor Mohr, Merry Christmas! You are certainly up early!
Mohr: Merry Christmas to you, Franz. Actually, I got very little sleep last night. You see, I wrote a poem. It's about the night our Savior was born. I call it "Silent Night, Holy Night."

Gruber: I see. And what may I do for you this beautiful Christmas morning?

Mohr: Would you be able to compose a tune to go along with my words? I know the organ is broken at church, so you can't use the organ. But, how about your guitar? I think it would be a lovely song for our Christmas service today.

Gruber: Today? Pastor, you are asking a lot! Well, I'll see what I can do.

Mohr: Thank you. *(He leaves the stage.)*

(Gruber sits down, picks up his guitar and begins strumming.)

Gruber: Hmm, let's see. "All is calm, all is bright." *(He continues working on the song for a bit.)* There! I think I've got it! *(He leaves the stage with guitar in hand.)*

(Child comes up on stage and rings bell.)

Child: Church time! Time for our Christmas service!

(All the children come up on stage.)

Mohr: Dear friends of our church, the Lord gave me a poem last evening as I thought about my journey up the mountain to see a new-born child. I gave the poem to our talented organist and choirmaster, Franz Gruber. God gave him the tune for this song in a few hours! We would like to sing it as a duet for you now.

Narrator: Pastor Joseph Mohr and his musician friend, Franz Gruber, sang "Silent Night" as a duet that Christmas day, 1818, in a small village of Austria. Today, it is known around the world as a worshipful carol of peace.

Song: "Silent Night! Holy Night!" *(Three verses with guitar accompaniment, if possible.)*

"O Little Town of Bethlehem"

Phillips Brooks

Act 1—Trip to the Holy Land

Brooks stands off to side of platform and waves to people sitting in pews.

Man *(stands up and says):* We're going to miss you, Pastor Brooks, but we hope you have a wonderful year of travel. You've earned it!

Brooks: Thank you, one and all! I will certainly miss all of you and my beloved Philadelphia.

Narrator: Months pass. Pastor Brooks travels all over Europe. He comes to the Holy Land in mid-December. He is thrilled to travel all over the land where Jesus lived while He was here on earth.

Brooks: Christmas Eve! Now is the time to visit Bethlehem. I think of Luke 2:4: "So Joseph also went up from the town of Galilee to Judea, to Bethlehem the town of David, because he belonged to the house and line of David." *(He looks around.)* Ah, yes! Everything is just as I pictured it. Bethlehem is really quite small. And here's a special Christmas Eve church service. I think I will go in. This is indeed a holy place.

Act 2—Writing The Carol

Props: paper, pencil, table, chair

Narrator: Pastor Brooks has been home for three years now. But, he still has many pictures in his mind of his travels all over the world. Bethlehem especially stands out.

Scene 1

Scene is set with table, chair, paper and pencil. A child is talking to Pastor Brooks.

Child: Pastor Brooks, could you write a Christmas song for the children to sing on Christmas day? It's a few weeks away.

Brooks: I could try, I guess. *(He sits down and begins to think and write for quite a while.)* There! That will work, I believe. *(Knock on the door.)* Come in.

Redner: Good morning, Pastor Brooks.

Brooks: Ah, Lewis Redner. Just the man I hoped to see. Here is a hymn I have just written. Why not write a new tune for it? The children are hoping to sing it on Christmas.

(Redner looks over the sheet of paper.)

Redner: I'll do my best. "O Little Town of Bethlehem."

Scene 2

Redner sits at his organ, writing, scratching out, throwing away papers, etc. Looks frustrated. There are chairs for a bed. Angelic sounding music from a piano is heard from offstage.

Redner: This is just not going well. I've tried and tried, but nothing seems right. And, it's Christmas Eve! I don't want to let down Pastor Brooks and the children! What am I going to do?

(He lies down on two chairs and sleeps. Suddenly, the piano plays angelic sounds—chords in the upper range. Redner sits up.)

Redner: What was that? It sounded like angels. Hmm. Hmm. *(He picks up a piece of paper and writes down the melody. Then he goes back to sleep. Pause. Redner wakes up and yawns.)*

Redner: Was that a dream in the night? Or did I really hear some angel sounds? *(He looks down and sees his paper.)* Well, the melody I wrote down still looks good. Yes, I know now what the harmony should sound like also. *(Redner rushes over to the side of the stage and calls.)* Pastor Brooks! Children! Everyone come, quickly! I finally have our new Christmas song!

(All the children come up on stage.)

Song: "O Little Town of Bethlehem" *(three verses)*

Conclusion

Narrator: It is fun to sing new songs at Christmas. But, the old ones came to us in such interesting ways, it is great to sing the traditional carols as well. Christmas is a time of honoring Christ's birth. God proved His love for us by sending His Son to earth.

Children *(quote John 3:16)*: "For God so loved the world that he gave his one and only Son, that whoever believes in him shall not perish but have eternal life."

Narrator: As you hear and sing the lovely old carols of Christmas, don't forget each one has a story behind it. The important thing is that they all highlight the miraculous birth of Jesus Christ, our Savior, who came to earth because He loves each one of us.

Closing remarks may be given by the narrator or other designated person.

###

Bainton, Roland H., *Here I Stand: A Life of Martin Luther,* New American Library, 1950.

Emurian, Ernest K., *Living Stories of Famous Hymns*, Interlude Books, Baker Book House, 1955.

The Wish

Dolores Steger

A Christmas play in three acts for children of all ages.

Characters and Costumes:
Mother—housedress for Act 1, night robe for Act 3
Child—nightclothes (A name may be given the Child)
Mary—dressed in robe and mantle
Joseph—dressed in sashed robe
Innkeeper—dressed in sashed robe
Shepherds—dressed in robes; bandannas on heads (any number of
    "Shepherds" may participate, two have speaking parts)
Three Kings—dressed in robes; crowns on heads
Angel—dressed in white robe

Set Requirements:

(manger set up as in past – "living room" on front stage)

Set elements remain stationary throughout the play; Acts 1 and 3 take
    place in the Present, in the living room of a home; Act 2 takes place
    in the stable at the time of Jesus' birth.
Front stage right is set, simply, as the living room: Required: 2 chairs
Optional: other "living room" furnishings; Christmas tree; packages
Front stage left is set as the stable: Required: 2 chairs; basket/manger
Optional: Other elements of the manger scene

Props: Representation of the baby Jesus (doll), small blanket to wrap
    the "baby," three gifts for the Magi, Bible
Music: Choir or Tape
Scripture: Luke 2, Matthew 2, The New International Version

Act 1—Christmas Eve Present

SS sing

*Music plays "Away in a Manger." Mother and Child are seated in the
living room; Mother is reading from the Bible; music continues to play
softly in the background until Mother stops reading.*
Mother: *(Reads Luke 2:1-7)* *from Bible*
Child: I love that story!
Mother: Yes, it is beautiful!
Child: I wish I could have been by the manger to see the birth of the
    Son of God.

Mother *(nodding):* It must have been wonderful, but we have the Bible
    to tell us all about it; that makes us feel as if we were there. And,
    tomorrow we celebrate Jesus' birth, just as we do every Christmas.
    That, too, reminds us of how our Lord came to be with us.

Child: Yes, but I still wish . . .

Mother: Right now, you'll have to do your wishing and your praying in
    bed. It's getting late and we want to be ready for Jesus' birthday cele-
    bration at church tomorrow.

*(Music plays "Hark! the Herald Angels Sing." Mother and Child rise;
Mother puts arm around Child's shoulder and both exit, stage right.
Music plays through one verse of the hymn; at the start of the second
verse, Angel enters rear stage left and walks slowly to stage right. Music
stops as Angel speaks, calling offstage, stage right.)*

Angel *(softly):* Child! Child! Wake up! Come here! Wake up!

(Child enters, rubbing eyes and appearing half asleep.)

Angel: So, you heard me! You're here! Good! Come, now! We must be off!

Child: Off? To where? Who are you?

Angel: Look at me! Who do you think I am? You prayed and made a
    wish and I'm here to see that you get it!

Child: A wish?

Angel: Yes! Don't you remember? The manger? The birth of the Son of
    God?

Child: But—but . . . This must be a dream!

Angel: If you want to be there, we must hurry! It's soon time!

Child: But—but . . .

*(Music plays "Silent Night! Holy Night!" Angel takes Child's hand and
both walk slowly across stage toward manger scene. Mary and Joseph
enter and seat themselves in chairs at the scene.)*

SS and Congregation sing →

Act 2—A Stable in Bethlehem

after Song

~~Music continues playing.~~ *Angel and Child stand near the scene. Mary is
wrapping the "baby Jesus" in a blanket. Innkeeper enters rear stage
right and approaches scene; music stops as Innkeeper speaks.*

Innkeeper *(to Mary and Joseph):* Sorry there was no room at the inn. The
    census, you know. Bethlehem is very crowded, but you and the Baby
    seem to be doing fine here. *(Mary and Joseph nod and smile.)* Send for
    me if there is anything I can do for you or if you need something. *(Mary
    and Joseph nod and smile again; Innkeeper exits stage left.)*

Child: I remember that part of the story.

Angel: Yes! "While they were there, the time came for the baby to be
    born, and she gave birth to her firstborn, a son. She wrapped him in

cloths and placed him in a manger, because there was no room for them in the inn."

Sing (Music plays "Silent Night! Holy Night!" Shepherds enter rear stage right and move to manger scene; as they approach, music subsides and Child speaks.)

Child (pointing to shepherds): Look! Here come the shepherds.

Angel: The angel told them to come, you know! "This will be a sign to you: You will find a baby wrapped in cloths and lying in a manger."

Child: And the shepherds listened and came! They really came!

(Shepherds bow before the "Baby.")

Shepherd 1: We have come to "see this thing that has happened, which the Lord has told us about."

Shepherd 2: We are amazed! We have come to worship this baby!
(Mary and Joseph smile and nod. Shepherds continue to bow and pray.)

Child: See how the shepherds are bowing and praying! When they leave, I know just what they're going to do!

Angel: Yes! They will "spread the word concerning what had been told them about this child."

Child: And everyone will be as amazed as the shepherds were. (Angel nods.) → Piano Only

Sing (Music plays "While Shepherds Watched Their Flocks." Shepherds exit, slowly, stage right, one or two at a time. Music plays until all Shepherds leave and subsides as Child speaks.)

Child (pointing to Mary and Joseph): They're alone now. It's really quiet. I think the baby is sleeping.

Angel (nodding): And Mary is treasuring "up all these things . . . in her heart."

(Angel and Child continue to look at nativity scene. Wise men enter rear stage right, singing "We Three Kings of Orient Are." Substitute tape/choir, if necessary. They appear to be pointing toward a star in the sky as they move to the manger scene. Child speaks when the Wise men reach the scene and stop singing.)

Child: Take a look at them! Look at the robes and the crowns! Awesome! ⟍ Congregation

Angel: Indeed!

Child: They must be very rich!

Angel: Oh, yes!

Child: Will they do what the Bible story says they did?

Angel: Let's watch and see!

King 1 (approaches manger, kneels, presents his gift): I bring you, Baby King, the gift of incense, sweet of scent, though far less sweet than You! (King 1 leaves his gift and stands.)

King 2 *(following the lead of King 1):* For you, tiny Ruler, I offer my gift of myrrh, comforting to the touch, as comforting as You will come to be.

King 3 *(following the lead of Kings 1 and 2):* For you, King of kings, I have gold, shining and bright, but dimmed by Your light.

(All three kings are now standing.)

King 1 *(to Mary and Joseph):* We are honored to be in the presence of the Baby. *(Mary and Joseph smile and nod.)*

King 2: Yes, and we are sorry we must leave so soon. We have a very long journey.

King 3: Our journey will be longer because we must take a different route back to our homes. We were warned not to follow the same path we used when we came.

Child *(as Wise men wave to Mary and Joseph and exit, stage right):* It's true! Just like the Bible says!

Angel: Yes! "And having been warned in a dream . . . they returned to their country by another route." And, speaking of returning, it's time I take you back.

Child: Oh, must we go? I want to remember this moment forever!

Angel *(taking Child's hand, exiting slowly stage right as music plays "It Came upon the Midnight Clear"):* You will! You will!

Cong Sing

Act 3—Christmas Day Present

Music continues to play "It Came upon the Midnight Clear." Mother and Child enter the living room from stage right; music stops as Mother speaks.

Mother: You are up very early this Christmas morning. *(Child nods.)* To open your gifts?

Child: No, to get ready to celebrate the birth of Jesus. I'm really ready for it this year!

Mother: Oh?

Child: I know the story's true and I know just how it happened. My wish came true! I was there!

Mother: Of course you were! Everyone is there when they read God's word about it in the Bible and we did that only last night. Remember?

Child: I remember! I fell asleep thinking about it!

Mother: That's a wonderful way to fall asleep!

Child: It was as if I were right there at the time of Jesus' birth. Shepherds, Wise men, Mary and Joseph, the Innkeeper, the Angel—Yes! And, then, an Angel came and—Yes! I was really there! My wish came true!

Mother *(taking Child's hand and exiting stage right):* Oh! Amazing! Come! Tell me about it!

(Music plays "Joy to the World." All characters reenter for curtain call.)

Long Ago in Bethlehem

Lillian Robbins

A play in three scenes. A shorter play can be presented by using the last two scenes only with an appropriate introduction by the Narrator. The number of characters can be reduced if dialogue is combined for some of the travelers.

Characters:
Narrator
News Reporter
Six Travelers
Boy Helper
Merchant
Innkeeper
Joseph
Mary
Three Shepherds
Three Wise men
Speaking Angel
Singing Angels *(as many as you wish)*
Extras walking through street scene *(optional)*

Scene 1: Street of Bethlehem near the inn
Scene 2: Hillside near Bethlehem
Scene 3: Stable in Bethlehem

Props: Cordless microphone, crooks for shepherds, doll as baby Jesus, manger, straw, tote bag with supplies, spotlight, stumps or blankets for shepherds, three gifts, folded blanket

Clothes: Appropriate for characters of that time

Scene 1

Bethlehem on Christmas Eve.

Narrator: It may have been December 24th or some other date on the calendar of Israel long ago. No one knows the exact date of this remarkable event.

A decree had gone out from Caesar Augustus that all of the people must go to be taxed. On every road, down every path, across every hill, one may have seen men and women making their way to the home of their ancestors that they might obey the new law which was made known to the people of Israel.

Every detail of that special night is not recorded in the Bible. We can only imagine how it might have been. One may imagine what the comments would have been if a news reporter had stopped travelers to inquire about their opinions of the events taking place.

(Travelers walk on stage as dialogue is spoken.)

Reporter *(stops first traveler):* Excuse me, sir. Would you just let me speak with you for a moment about your travel to this city? Are you here for the taxing?

First Traveler: I sure am—been walking a long ways.

Reporter: What do you think about this Roman census?

First Traveler: Don't like it. It's not fair.

Reporter: But you are here to pay your taxes anyway.

First Traveler: I have no choice. It's the rule of the land. What else can a fellow do but obey the law? *(Exits.)*

Reporter *(stops another traveler):* Excuse me, sir. What do you think of the decree from Caesar Augustus that brings you here to Bethlehem?

Second Traveler: I'm far too busy to take all this time to come to Bethlehem. I have a lot more important things to do. *(Exits.)*

Reporter *(stops another traveler)*: Excuse me, Sir. You seem to be in a hurry.

Third Traveler: I got work to do. Far too busy to have to come to Bethlehem to bother with taxes.

Reporter: Bethlehem looks pretty crowded. Do you think you'll be able to get room for the night?

Third Traveler *(disgruntled):* I don't know. *(Exits.)*

Reporter *(stops merchant):* You don't really look like a traveler. Do you live here in Bethlehem?

Merchant *(smiling broadly):* Oh, yes! Bethlehem is my home. It's a great time here for merchants like me.

Reporter: Then you approve of the command by the government that all these people come back to Bethlehem for the census?

Merchant: That I do. Nothing sounds better than the jingle of coins in my pocket. Even fellows like you buy something while they are here. *(Chuckles and exits.)*

Reporter *(to himself):* I guess he's right about that. *(Stops another traveler.)* What do you think about this taxing business?

Fourth Traveler: Don't like it. Don't like to pay it. Don't like to have to come here. Don't like anything about it. And the least those Romans could have done for our people would have been to let us list taxes in our own hometown.

Reporter: But how could that have been accomplished?

Fourth Traveler: It would be easy. The government could have sent somebody to the little towns where the people live all across Israel to take the census and collect the taxes. Then we wouldn't have had to come all this way.

Reporter: Why do you think Caesar Augustus didn't think of that?

Fourth Traveler: He doesn't care. He just wants our money. I have to go. *(Exits.)*

Reporter *(sops another traveler):* Excuse me, sir. I was just wondering, what do you think about the rooming situation in Bethlehem at a time like this? Do you think you'll be able to get a room?

Fifth Traveler: I'm not worried. I got here early. Already got my place.

Reporter: You know the inns could get full. Would you be willing to share your space or give it up to somebody else?

Fifth Traveler: Why should I? Let everybody look after himself. *(Exits.)*

Reporter *(to himself):* You meet all kinds of people at a time like this. *(Knocks on door of inn, Innkeeper opens door.)*

Innkeeper: What can I do for you?

Reporter: I'm a news reporter, talking to some of the people who have traveled to Bethlehem for the taxing. Do you think you are going to have enough room to accommodate all these visitors in your town?

Innkeeper: I don't know how we can. Almost every space is full now.

Reporter: What in the world will people do if they can't find lodging?

Innkeeper: Don't know.

Sixth Traveler *(arrives with two others):* We need rooms for the night.

Innkeeper: Come on in. We'll see what we can do. *(Exits.)*

Reporter *(to boy coming on stage carrying folded blanket):* Just a minute young man. You seem to be in a hurry.

Boy: I am. The boss is keeping me on the go all the time. I have to fetch more blankets, fetch more pillows, fetch more water, fetch more food. It's just too much work. *(He hurries on.)*

Reporter *(stops Joseph):* You look like a traveler in Bethlehem. Are you here for the taxing?

Joseph: Yes, I'm Joseph of the line of David.

Reporter: What do you think about the decree from Rome?

Joseph: Sorry, can't talk with you now. I must hurry to get a room for my wife.

Reporter: Suppose there is no room.

Joseph: God will provide. *(Knocks on door, Innkeeper comes out.)* I need room for the night.

Innkeeper: Sorry, there is no more room.

Joseph: But there must be! My wife is weary and must have a place to rest.

Innkeeper: But what can I do? Those men took the last space.

Joseph: There must be some place. My wife is going to give birth to her firstborn child. It may be born tonight.

Innkeeper: Well, how about if you go down to the stable? You could use clean straw and make her a bed there.

Joseph: We'll do that. Thank you for your kindness. *(Joseph hurries away.)*

Reporter *(speaking to himself):* Some of these people may have a hard time in Bethlehem. There are so many people and not enough room for them. *(Sees boy hurrying across stage.)* Wait a minute, there.

Boy: I can't. I must hurry to get fresh straw.

Reporter: But you don't have the same weary look you had when I spoke to you before.

Boy: But the lady needs me. She must have fresh straw for a bed right away. And Joseph needs fresh straw in the manger to make a bed for the baby. I must hurry. *(Exits.)*

Reporter *(stops shepherd who is carrying bag):* You there. It seems strange to see a shepherd here among all these travelers.

Shepherd: I just had to get a few supplies. But I must hurry back to my flock. I feel a pressing need to be there on that hillside. *(Exits.)*

Reporter: I just wonder what will happen before this night is over.

Scene 2

On hillside. Two shepherds sit on stumps or ground.

Narrator: And there were in the same country shepherds abiding in the field, keeping watch over their flocks by night.

First Shepherd: Here comes Stephen. It didn't take him long to get back from town. *(Stephen enters.)*

Second Shepherd *(Shepherds stand):* How was it in town today?

Stephen *(drops bag on ground):* Busy. There were so many people from everywhere. I could hardly get around the crowds. I rushed so much I'm really tired. *(Reclines on blanket.)*

First Shepherd: But you chose to be the one to go for supplies.

Stephen: I know, but I'm tired now.

Second Shepherd: Did you get the bread?

Stephen: Sure I did.

First Shepherd: What about that ointment I need?

Stephen: Got that, too.

(Pause as shepherds remove items from bag.)

Narrator: "And, lo, the angel of the Lord came upon them, and the glory of the Lord shone round about them; and they were sore afraid. *(Bright light as angel appears. Shepherds fall to their knees.)* And the angel said unto them, Fear not: for, behold, I bring you good tidings of great joy, which shall be to all people. For unto you is born this day in the city of David a Saviour, which is Christ the Lord. And this shall be a sign unto you; Ye shall find the babe wrapped in swaddling clothes, lying in a manger. *(A host of angels appears.)* And suddenly there was with the angel a multitude of the heavenly host praising God, and saying, Glory to God in the highest, and on earth peace, good will toward men."

Angels *(in unison)*: Glory to God! Glory to God! Glory to God in the highest! *(Angels sing * "Glory to God" by Lister or another appropriate song, then exit.)*

First Shepherd *(as they rise from their knees)*: I never expected to see an angel from God.

Second Shepherd: And not just one. There were so many of them. They just appeared from nowhere.

First Shepherd: And where did they go?

Stephen: What do you think it all means?

Second Shepherd: Why would an angel come to speak to us? We're just shepherds.

Stephen: Well, you heard what the angel said about a baby being born in the city of David. There really was a lot going on in Bethlehem today.

First Shepherd: Do you think we could find this baby the angel spoke about?

Second Shepherd: A baby lying in a manger? That would be unusual.

Stephen: And the angel said it is Christ the Lord.

(Shepherds quietly talk among themselves.)

Narrator: "The shepherds said one to another, Let us now go even unto Bethlehem, and see this thing which is come to pass, which the Lord hath made known unto us." *(Shepherds exit.)*

Scene 3

Stable—Mary and Joseph on stage—baby in manger.

Narrator: Mary gave birth to her firstborn son. There was no room in the inn, but God did provide. There in the humble abode of the animals,

Jesus was born. His bed was a manger from which the animals had eaten their food. But surely Mary and Joseph must have thanked God for the safe journey from Nazareth to Bethlehem and for the opportunity to go into the stable for shelter.

It didn't seem like the place for a king to be born. And a peasant virgin from Nazareth may not have appeared to be a proper mother for the King, but God chose that it should be so. And Mary kept all these things in her heart.

The shepherds came to the stable to visit this one who was born to be the Savior of the world. "And they came with haste, and found Mary and Joseph, and the babe lying in a manger." *(Shepherds come forward and bow before the manger. Singing of "Silent Night! Holy Night!" is heard from backstage.)*

Narrator: "And when they had seen it, they made known abroad the saying which was told them concerning this child."

(Shepherds exit. Mary picks up the baby and sings "Away in a Manger.")

Narrator: When the wise men from the east followed the star all the way to Bethlehem, they, too, were able to visit the Christ Child. The time of their arrival is not certain, but it is certain that they came and brought gifts: gold, frankincense, and myrrh.

(Kings come forward, place gifts in front of manger, kneel. Singing off stage. "O Come, All Ye Faithful" or "We Three Kings of Orient Are.")

Narrator: And so the baby Jesus was visited by lowly shepherds and royalty from afar. This most special moment that history has ever known from the creation of the world has brought joy to the hearts of multitudes of people, beginning in Bethlehem and spreading throughout the world.

Optional: *(Cast assembles and sings "Joy to the World.")*

Narrator: And may the peace and joy of Christmas fill your hearts as you experience anew the great miracle of the birth of Jesus, the only begotten Son of God. May we pray together. *(Brief prayer to close.)*

*Song, "Glory to God" from *Name Above All Names* arranged by Mosie Lister, published by Lillenas.

Scriptures from Luke 2, King James Version.

The Reason for the Season

Linda A. and John Wurzbacher

Speaking Parts:
Gabrielle
Michael
Jason
David
Brenda
Karen
VOICE
Shepherds—2
Wise men—3
Angel Sara
Scripture Readers—8 children

Non speaking Parts:
Mary
Joseph

Props needed: four book bags, plants, three gifts—one a bag of gold, manger scene, time machine. Time machine can be made from a large refrigerator box. It needs to be large enough for four children to fit into. Should have a light bulb on top and make strange chiming sounds. Let the children use their imaginations to create something spectacular.

Scene 1

Gabrielle: Welcome friends, we are angels.
Michael: Messengers of God.
Gabrielle: You may have already known that, since angels are mentioned in the Bible over 300 times!
Michael: We have been in your church many times before, though you may not have seen us.
Gabrielle: Some of you have even entertained us as strangers, though you were unaware.
Michael: The children have asked us here today to help them tell you a story.
Gabrielle: It happened only last week. But the children are very excited.
Michael: Yes, and they have good reason to be excited. They have had quite a . . . how do you say that Gabrielle, awwesome experience?
Gabrielle: Yes Michael, they said awwwesome!

Michael: It all started with these four children who, sadly to say, knew very little about the true meaning of Christmas.

Gabrielle *(with hand at side of his mouth)*: Their parents never taught them about God or took them to church!

Michael: That's true Gabrielle. They thought Christmas was about getting toys and toys and . . . toys and . . . more toys.

Gabrielle *(hand at side of mouth again):* Sadly, some adults think that too.

Michael: Gabrielle!

(Gabrielle shrugs with hands held up.)

Michael: Anyway, these children were on their way home from school one day when they stumbled onto something pretty amazing. Take it away kids.

(Two boys walk in carrying book bags, talking to each other.)

Jason: How did you do on your math test?

David: Not too good. I didn't understand it.

Jason: I hurried through mine so I could have time to work on my Christmas list.

David: My list has been done for a month! All I want is a 32X video machine.

Jason: You're out of your mind, that costs $150.00! My parents would never get that for me.

David: Well, I thought I could . . . *(David sees the time machine.)* WOW!!! Jason look!!! What IS that thing?????

Jason: WOW!!!

(Both boys are silent for a moment, stare and look in wonder at machine.)

Jason: What is that thing?

David: I don't know. It's weird looking!

(Two girls, carrying book bags, come on stage from the same direction the boys did.)

Brenda: Hi guys, what's up?

Karen: Hey, what is that thing?

(Brief silence as all children look it over in amazement.)

Jason: We don't know; we just found it here.

David: It looks like some kind of machine.

Brenda: Open the door.

(David tries to open the door and can't.)

Jason: It's stuck.

Karen: I see a button by the door.

Brenda: Push it David. Maybe it opens the door.

(David pushes button and hears a strange musical tone, then a deep voice.)

VOICE: Welcome! I am the GATEWAY.

Karen: Gateway? *(Sounding scared.)*

VOICE: Fear not! For I am the gateway to the Good News.

David: What good news?

VOICE: The true meaning of Christmas. Step inside and I will transport you back in time.

Jason: IT'S A TIME MACHINE!!!!

Brenda: COOL!

Karen: AWESOME!

Jason: WOW!

David: Let's go!

Karen *(acting scared):* I don't know about this guys. I have a lot of homework.

Brenda: Come on Karen, it's a time machine!

Jason: Where did you say we were going?

VOICE: Back in time to a little town called Bethlehem.

Karen: Bethlehem? Where's that? *(Asking Brenda.)*

Brenda: I don't know. I got a D in geography.

David: Let's go!

(All four kids get inside time machine and close door. Congregation sings first verse of "O Come, All Ye Faithful.")

Scene 2

Scenery looks like Bethlehem did in Bible times, needs to include some large plants. A light bulb lights up on top of machine. Strange chiming sounds are heard. Time machine rocks slightly. Kids inside make oohing and aahing sounds. Kids step outside, look around in amazement.

Jason: Where are we?

David: This place looks old!

Brenda: Sshhhh! I hear someone coming.

(Children hide behind plants. From right enter three shepherds talking very quickly and excitedly to each other, unaware that the children are there.)

Shepherd 1: I didn't know what to think. I was so scared at first.

Shepherd 2: Me too! I mean it's not every day that angels appear to you.

Shepherd 3: There was a whole crowd of them too!

Shepherd 1: Why did they pick us to appear to?

Shepherd 2: I know. We're just lowly shepherds. Nobody cares about shepherds. We smell too much like our sheep.

Shepherd 3: I didn't know what to say. What can you say to an angel!

Shepherd 1: I was too scared to say anything.

Shepherd 2: I don't think he wanted us to say anything. He just wanted us to go.

Shepherd 3: I'll never forget what he said to us: I am bringing you good news of great joy . . . for to you is born . . . a savior.

Shepherd 1: I'm so glad we listened and went to that stable.

Shepherd 2: I am too.

Shepherd 3: I am going to tell everyone the good news.

Shepherd 1: Yes! Let's go tell our families. They will be so excited!

Shepherd 2: That was quite an experience in that stable. . . . *(Shepherd 2's voice almost fades off as they disappear and walk off on opposite side they entered.)*

(Children come out from behind plants looking at each other in wonder. Talk excitedly and fast.)

David: Wow! Did you hear what they said?

Brenda: Angels? They saw real angels?

Karen: We really are back in time. Did you catch the duds they had on?

Jason: They did smell like their sheep. WOW! *(Waves hand in front of face.)*

David: They said an angel appeared in the sky and told them about a savior?

Jason: What is a savior anyway?

Brenda: I don't know. I got a D in vocabulary too.

David: I remember when I went to church with my cousins once and they talked about Jesus being the Savior.

Karen: My grandmother told me once that Jesus is the son of God. She said God came to earth as a man to save us from our sins.

Brenda: Our sins?

Karen: Yeah, she said like when we do things like not obeying God and hurting other people.

Jason: WOW! We have a lot to learn about the true meaning of Christmas. I thought it was just about Santa Claus and getting lots of presents.

David: We should tell our parents to take us to church.

Brenda: SShhh!!! I hear more people coming.

(Children duck behind plants again. Congregation sings first and second verses of "We Three Kings of Orient Are." Three wise men walk in talking to each other.)

Wise man 1: Look! I can see the place! The star is above that house. Finally, we will see the young king!

Wise man 2: Finally, we can give Him our gifts!

Wise man 3: I knew that star would lead us to Him.

Wise man 1: Hurry my friends. Our long journey is finally over.
Wise man 2: At last!
Wise man 3: The priests were right! I knew it!
Wise man 1: Hurry!
(As the Wise men rush off Wise man #2 drops his bag of gold. Children rush out and Jason picks it up.)
Brenda: What is it?
Jason: WOW! We're rich! It's real gold!
(All children say wow and want to touch it.)
Karen: Think of all the Christmas presents we can buy with it!
David: We can't keep it.
Jason: What? Finders keepers, David!
Brenda: He's right Jason, that present belongs to the king!
Jason: What king?
David: The king those guys have been looking for. I think it's Jesus.
Karen: Jesus is the king? Oh Jason, we have to give it back.
Jason: Well, they're long gone. How do we find this king?
Brenda: We do what they did. We follow the star.
David: Yeah! *(Looks and points to the star.)* It can't be too far, let's go!
Karen: Let's follow that star!!

Song: "We Three Kings of Orient Are" *(last three verses)*

Scene 3

The manger scene. Children enter from back. Wise man 2 is sitting in front of manger with his head in his hands.

David: Look, that star is shining right down on that house!
Jason: Yeah, and the guy who dropped his gold is sitting outside.
Brenda: Let's go!
(Children walk up to Wise man 2.)
Karen: Sir, are you crying?
(Wise man looks up and then puts head back in his hands.)
Wise man 2: Yes children. I have journeyed far to see the newborn King and somehow I have lost the gift I brought for him.
David: We found your gift and brought it to you.
(David hands Wise man 2 gift. Wise man 2 stands up and holds bag of gold up toward sky.)
Wise man 2: Oh, thank you children. Now I can go in and see the KING! Why don't you come with me?
Karen: Yeah. I want to see the King!

(The Wise man and children enter the manger scene. Other two Wise men are there on knees before Jesus with gifts in front of them, praying. Wise man 2 falls down to knees next to them and worships Him.)

Little Children: "Away in a Manger"
(The children go over and look in cradle. Then step back. Gabrielle and David come over to children. There is soft music that sounds like angels are singing.)

Gabrielle: Children, Fear not! I am Gabrielle, God's messenger. Blessed are your eyes for what they have seen. For today all in Heaven rejoice!

Brenda: Gabrielle, is that Jesus? *(To be said very timidly.)*

Gabrielle: Yes! "For God so loved the world that he gave his one and only Son, that whoever believes in him shall not perish but have eternal life." This is the Good News of great joy for every person. Today the Savior of the world has been born.

(The children fall to their knees, bow their heads in worship. Congregation sings "Joy to the World!" Children rise after singing. Walk back to front of the time machine.)

Karen: Wow! This was an awesome experience.

Jason: Awesome!

David: I didn't know this is what Christmas is really about.

Brenda: I wonder why our parents didn't tell us.

Jason: I don't think they know. It's up to us to tell them. We need to learn more about Jesus.

Karen: Now I think I understand why kids go to Sunday school. To learn more about Jesus. They are *so* lucky!

David: But there are lots of kids who *don't* go to Sunday school! Maybe we should tell them about Jesus!

Brenda: Yeah, I think many grown-ups have forgotten what Christmas is really about too. We should tell everyone.

Jason: I hear lots of people say Jesus' name when they are angry. We should tell them that's wrong.

Karen: Let's spread the word. **Jesus is the reason for the season!**

All Kids: Yeah! **Jesus is the reason for the season!**

David: Yeah! Let's go back and tell everyone!!!!

(Children get back into time machine. Congregation sings refrain of "Let Jesus Come into Your Heart.")

Scene 4

Angels return to microphone.

Gabrielle: Well, friends, there you have it. Quite an awesome experience they had.

Michael: Awwesomme!

Gabrielle: There's much to be learned by what the children have . . .

(Angel Sara walks up to Gabrielle with a letter in hand.)

Angel Sara: Excuse me, Gabrielle.

Gabrielle: Yes Sara, what is it?

Angel Sara: A letter just arrived for you.

Gabrielle: Why thank you Sara.

(Sara remains standing next to Gabrielle.)

Michael: I didn't know angels could get letters.

Gabrielle: Look Michael, it's from the children.

Michael *(looking confused):* What kind of a stamp did they use?

Gabrielle: Sara, please do us the honor and read us the letter.

Angel Sara: Sure Gabrielle. It says,

Dear Gabrielle and Michael:

Thank you for helping us share our story about our awesome experience. We want you to know that we did go back and tell our families, friends and neighbors. Some listened and started to read the Bible and go to church. And they in turn told even more people. The good news brought great joy and peace to many people, just like you said. Sometimes it was hard to share our story because a few people laughed at us and made fun of us. They thought we were weird! But Karen's grandma told us to pray for them anyway and not get discouraged. She showed us in the Bible where it said that God wanted each one of us to keep on spreading the word about Jesus so that everyone would have a chance to know the true meaning of Christmas and what it means for every single one of us. She also showed us where it said God would be there to help and guide us. Thanks for all your help. Now we can understand why you are called God's messengers. We hope we too, in some small way, can also be God's messengers. Merry Christmas!

Love,
David, Jason, Brenda and Karen

Michael: What a beautiful letter.

Gabrielle: Beautiful. Thanks for reading it Sara.

(Sara smiles and walks away.)

Gabrielle: Well, Michael, our work here is done for now.

Michael: Yes, Gabrielle. We have an angels committee meeting in Heaven in just a few minutes. *(Looks at watch.)* You know the boss doesn't like it when we're late!

Gabrielle: Right Michael. But before we leave, let's ask the children to share some words from the Holy Book.

Michael: Yes. Children, please read.

Child 1: Psalm 100. "Shout for joy to the Lord, all the earth. Worship the Lord with gladness; come before him with joyful songs. Know that the Lord is God. It is he who made us, and we are his; we are his people, the sheep of his pasture.

Child 2: Enter his gates with thanksgiving and his courts with praise; give thanks to him and praise his name. For the Lord is good and his love endures forever; his faithfulness continues through all generations."

Child 3: Isaiah 63:7. "I will tell of the kindnesses of the Lord, the deeds for which he is to be praised, according to all the Lord has done for us—yes, the many good things he has done for the house of Israel, according to His compassion and many kindnesses."

Child 4: Colossians 3:12-14. "Therefore, as God's chosen people, holy and dearly loved, clothe yourselves with compassion, kindness, humility, gentleness and patience.

Child 5: "Bear with each other and . . . forgive as the Lord forgave you. And over all these virtues put on love, which binds them all together in perfect unity."

Child 6: From John 6:35. "I am the bread of life. He who comes to me will never go hungry, and he who believes in me will never be thirsty."

Child 7: From John 8:12. "I am the light of the world. Whoever follows me will never walk in darkness, but will have the light of life."

Child 8: From Matthew 28:19-20. "Therefore go and make disciples of all nations, baptizing them in the name of the Father and of the Son and of the Holy Spirit, and teaching them to obey everything I have commanded you. And surely, I am with you always, to the very end of the age."

PRAYER
CLOSING HYMN: "Go, Tell It on the Mountain"

Christmas Cousins

Sharon Kaye Kiesel

Cast:
Sarah and Jason *(siblings, not twins, ages 12-14)*
Father and Mother *(played by adults or older teens)*
Heather and Brian *(friends of Sarah and Jason, Heather not dressed as stylish as other three)*
Cousins *(10 children, assorted sizes and gender, ages 3 to 16)*

Props and settings:
Scene 1: Living room: couch, easy chair, coffee and end tables, telephone *(offstage ringer)*, partially decorated Christmas tree, box of decorations, stack of mail for mom. Optional: painted backdrop of wall and curtained window. *(Could paint backdrop for scene two on back and turn around for scene change.)*
Scene 2: Town square. Could have painted backdrop of decorated shops. Or: use tree from Scene 1 and drape garlands around stage area along with any desired indoor or outdoor decorations. Also need a three piece outdoor manger scene.
Optional: Live actors for Mary and Joseph, doll and manger for Jesus.
Scene 3: Living room: tree in corner, lots of colorful packages under it. All furniture pushed to outer edges of stage area. Center stage area carpeted with sleeping bags and bedrolls. *(Girls can be on one side, boys on the other.)*

Scene 1

Father, Jason and Sarah decorating the tree. Mother enters later.

Jason *(putting ornament on tree)*: I've just got to get that bike for Christmas. I *need* it. My knees keep hitting the handlebars on my old one.
Sarah *(laughing)*: Well, we always know where you are. We just listen for the thunka, thunka, thunka, ouch!
Jason *(making face)*: I didn't know you could hear anything. You're always chomping on a wad of gum.
Sarah: Well, I won't have to listen to you at all when I get my new Walkman.
Jason: If you get it. Anyway, if I don't get my bike, I'll be walkin' man.
Father *(clearing throat)*: I do believe you two have forgotten something . . . like there are more important things at Christmas than getting

presents. How about trying to get along? And what are you *giving* for Christmas, besides giving me a headache. *(Grimaces, rubbing head in mock pain.)*

Sarah: Oh Daddy, we do get along, most of the time. But I'll try harder. Hey! I won't argue with Jason for the rest of the year, if I can get that designer sweater I've been wanting. It's still on display in Jamison's Clothing Store window.

Jason *(staring, mouth open)*: You, won't argue with me, for . . . the rest of the year? HA! Some deal. That's only a couple more weeks.

Sarah: So? Bet you can't do it.

Jason: I can too.

Sarah: Can't.

Father: My, my children. How would you like to sit in a corner?

(The three laugh and begin to toss tinsel at each other. Mother enters with a handful of mail, looks at her family. Shakes her head.)

Mother: You throw it, you clean it up.

Father: Sorry Hon. Jason and Sarah were *not* arguing.

(Sarah and Jason begin picking up the mess.)

Mother *(picks tinsel from father's shirt)*: Yes, I can see that. *(She sits on couch.)* Listen, all of you. Oh! I'm so excited, I hardly know where to begin!

Father: Well, I'd say you were beginning to read the mail. Good news?

Mother *(holding up letter)*: Yes! This came. It's from my parents. They want to come and spend Christmas with us!

Jason *(leaning over mother's shoulder, reading letter)*: Grandma and Grandpa are coming? All right! Hey Sarah, Amy and Ruthie are coming too!

Sarah *(joining Jason)*: Really? We haven't seen them since last summer. It'll be fun. Mom, I know they're my aunts but they seem more like my sisters than yours.

Mother: Since they are only a few years older than you, I can see why. Is it okay then? For them to come?

Sarah, Father and Jason *(not together)*: Yeah! Sure! It'll be great. We can't wait!

Mother: Then you'll all help me get the house cleaned and get things ready?

(Long pause, then all laugh.)

Father: Don't worry, we'll all help.

Mother: Jason, you'll have to let Grandma and Grandpa have your room. And Sarah, we'll get a couple of cots. Amy and Ruthie can sleep in with you.

Jason: Than I get to sleep out here in my sleeping bag. Cool!

Sarah: And see all the presents before we do? No way! That's not fair!

Father *(gives warning look)*: Sarah. Exactly what color is that sweater?

Sarah (grinning): Got it Dad and it's blue, with white trim.

(She and Jason go back to tree decorating. Dad picks up a box just as the phone rings.)

Mother (answering phone): Hello? Oh, Mom! What, (Looks shocked.) Oh . . . well . . . yes. Sure it's okay. Yes, yes! (She smiles.) Around midnight? Yes, we'll be watching for you. Bye. (Slowly hangs up phone.)

Father: What's the matter? Is something wrong?

Mother: Yes! No! Oh . . . I mean . . . They're all coming! Oh dear! Where are we going to put everyone?

Jason: Grandma and Grandpa are still coming aren't they?

Mother: Why yes. But so is my brother and his wife, my sister and her husband and all your cousins . . . All of them!

Sarah: Mom! Counting us, that's eight grown-ups and twelve kids. Where are we all going to sleep?

Mother (counting on fingers): No . . . That's not right. Bobby and Jean just had twins.

Sarah (eyes to ceiling): Okay, fourteen kids. Where are we going to find enough beds?

Father: Sarah, your grandparents get your room. Jason, Bob, Jean and the twins get your room. Susan and Jim get ours. Mother and I will sleep on the sofa bed in the den. You kids will have to round up all the sleeping bags, blankets and pillows that you can find. We'll move the furniture around in here and all of you kids can rough it on the floor.

Jason: All right! A camp out! When are they coming Mom?

Mother: They'll be driving in two vans and leaving around noon. They should be here around midnight, Christmas Eve.

(Jason and Sarah, look dismayed.)

Sarah (wailing): Not on Christmas Eve!

Scene 2

Sarah, Jason, Brian and Heather are walking slowly on the town square, looking at all the decorations. Manger scene is last. Heather's clothing not as in style as other three.

Sarah: It's just not fair. I had plans for all my Christmas presents. I wanted the new all to myself. That's ruined now.

Jason: Same here. Now I'll have to share my new bike with my cousins. I suppose Benny will have to have a turn. He's so clumsy. He'll probably run into a tree and scratch the paint.

Brian: So let him ride your old bike.

Jason (disgusted): Great idea Brian! You don't know my cousins. They'll all want to ride the new bike. I'll be stuck riding the old one.

38

Brian: Well, if you don't get a new bike, there's no problem.

Jason: I don't want to think about that. I've *got* to get that bike.

Brian: If you do get it, what'll you do with the old one? After your cousins leave.

Jason: I don't know, sell it maybe . . .

Brian: Maybe we could fix it and donate it to the children's shelter. They can always use another bike.

Jason: Hmmm . . . We'll see. It all depends on what's left after my cousins get through with it.

Sarah: I'll say one thing . . . No one better touch my Walkman except me. Oh, and you Heather. Do you think you'll get that music tape you've been wanting?

Heather: I don't know. Mom's been working some overtime . . . but . . . there are some things we need first. The tape would be an extra expense. I haven't said too much. I'd hate for Mom to feel bad if she couldn't afford to get it for me

Brian *(rather arrogant):* It's only a tape. They don't cost *that* much!

(Heather looks away. Sarah gives Brian a warning look.)

Sarah *(quickly)*: What are you getting for Christmas, Bri?

Brian: I hope that new trivia game they've been advertising on TV. Dad said it's too expensive and for me to forget it. But he's said that so much, I'm sure I'm getting it. Hey! *(Walks backward, facing the others.)* I've got a question! *(Others groan. He ignores them.)*

Brian: Okay. Whose picture is on a ten dollar bill?

Jason: Sarah, can I have that ten dollars you owe me?

Sarah: What ten dollars?

(They laugh. By now they should be at the manger scene. They gaze quietly.)

Heather: It must have been so hard for people back then.

Sarah: I know. Today we can go so far and so fast, but back then Mary and Joseph had to walk wherever they went. The roads were narrow and rocky. Then, after they traveled all the way to Bethlehem, they were tired and hungry and the only place there was room for them was in a dirty old stable.

Brian: How could they have slept on that scratchy old hay?

Heather: What about the poor little baby? He was wrapped tight in strips of cloth. The poor thing probably couldn't move at all, then had to lay in a cow's feeding trough.

Jason *(shivering)*: At least all that hay and the animals' body heat helped keep that drafty stable warm. Boy Brian! Think how lucky your baby brother is . . . sleeping in a nice warm house. And all he has to smell is you! *(Playfully punches Brian on the arm.)*

Brian: Yeah. The only time he hears any braying is when *you* come over!

Jason *(wiggling fingers like ears over head)*: Heee . . . Haww!

Sarah: All right children. Think about it seriously. We are pretty lucky you know. We've all got warm houses, nice warm beds, plenty to eat . . . I don't know how people lived back then.

Brian: For Mary and Joseph it was only temporary. But people did have it harder then we do today and they survived. If they hadn't, we wouldn't be here now.

Sarah: I can't help thinking about poor Mary. They had to go away, to make the long journey to Bethlehem. You know how happy Mom is that her mom and dad are coming for Christmas? I'll bet when Mary left, she wondered if she'd ever see her parents again.

Heather: That's right. And didn't Mary and Joseph have to take Jesus into Egypt to save Him from Herod? It had to be years before they could go home and see their families.

Jason: I guess we are lucky. Our family lives over 600 miles away but we get to see them every summer.

Heather: It must be nice to have a big family. At home, there's just Mom and me.

Jason: Yeah, but you don't have to share everything with anyone, unless you want to.

Heather: If I had a brother or sister or even cousins, I'd want to share. I think it'd be fun to have others around.

Brian: You should have a baby brother who cries at night. Or a little sister who comes into your room without asking and gets into all your things. I don't have any privacy at all.

Jason: Heather, you come on over Christmas day. It'll be crazy around there. I'll bet you'd change your mind pretty quick.

Heather: Someday Brian, your brother and sister will grow up. And Jason, your cousins are only coming for Christmas, they're not moving in forever. You and Sarah are so blessed to have a family who loves you so much.

(Sarah and Jason look puzzled.)

Sarah: What do you mean?

Heather: Mom and I have family. They live ten miles away in Wellsville. I've never met my grandmother. I don't even know if I have cousins or not. Years ago, someone got mad at someone else and now no one's speaking to any of the others. But in your family, everyone seems to get along. They love you enough to travel hundreds of miles to spend Christmas with you. They probably had to change all their plans just to be able to come and see you.

Jason: I never thought of it like that.

Sarah: Me either. I wonder if our cousins feel the same way? After all, they're having to give up their Christmas Eve and be crowded in a couple of vans for a long, long time to get here. I wonder how they'll get their presents?

Brian: Yeah! I wonder if they are worried they'll have to share with you!

Sarah *(thoughtfully)*: Maybe presents aren't so important. I really do want to see my aunts and cousins. It would be kind of fun to show them around town. And you guys will get to meet all of them.

Jason: Maybe it'll stay cold enough we can go skating on the pond or sledding over on Wolfe's Hill.

Brian: That sounds like fun. I'll bring some marshmallows.

Heather: I can bake some cookies.

Sarah: Let's do it!

(They walk off discussing plans.)

Scene 3

Living room furniture around sides. Tree in corner with packages under-neath. Wall to wall sleeping bags and bedrolls. All kids enter talking about Christmas, etc. They find their places as they call out good night to Mom, Dad, Uncle Bobby, Aunt Susan and to each other. After they get settled, Sarah and Jason enter, rolled sleeping bags under their arms.

Jason *(looking around)*: Wow! Wall to wall cousins. Isn't it great? Heather really made me think. I guess we really *are* blessed to have a family as great as ours.

Sarah: I know. Even though we don't see these guys more than once or twice a year, it'd sure be lonesome without them. Just knowing they're there makes me feel good inside. People are really lots more important than presents. You know something? I don't care if I get that Walkman or not. I'd rather listen to Amy and Ruthie and the other girls anyway.

Jason: I feel the same way about the bicycle. I mean, I do need it, espe-cially since it'll increase my chance of getting a part-time job after school. And you know I'll share it with the cousins. But it's going to be a lot more fun playing football with the guys or going sledding with everyone.

Sarah: We were being sort of selfish, weren't we? I prayed about it and I truly don't feel resentful any more. There's a lot of love around here.

Jason *(grinning)*: Yeah! That's 'cause there isn't room for anything else!

(They settle. Children resume talk about Christmas etc.)

Father *(enters room, exasperated)*: Okay gang! Quiet! Look, it's almost Christmas. I'd sure like to have a silent night for what's left of it. PLEASE?

(Kids hush. Father leaves. Kids giggle, then sit up and get serious before singing one verse of "Silent Night." At end of verse and chorus, Sarah, Jason or song leader invites audience to join in and sing the remaining verses.)

Just Something for Jesus

Lillian Robbins

Characters:
Mr. Fred *(an adult or child made up to look like an old man)*
Sarah
Melinda
Katrina
Katrina's mother
Tamra
Gary
Mrs. Knight
Sidney
Ashley
Charles
Sam
Boy *(wears torn jeans)*
Little Stephanie

Scene 1: Outside cabin—before Christmas
Scene 2: Outside cabin—Christmas Eve

Props: Bench, wood, knife, packages from shopping, cordless mike, doll, wheelchair, cookies, handmade Christmas card, jeans, jacket, quarters, little box for collections, wig or other make up for old man. *(Some mike arrangement for children's voices to be heard, perhaps mike hidden in bush beside bench.)*

Scene 1

Outside cabin—before Christmas Day. Mr. Fred sits on bench whittling.

Sarah *(enters)*: Hey, mister. What are you doing?
Mr. Fred: Just whittling.
Sarah: Somebody told me you give good advice.
Mr. Fred: What can I help you with?
Sarah: It's almost Christmas and I want to give something to Jesus for His birthday, but I don't know what to do about it.
Mr. Fred: Well, let me see. *(Pauses, thinking.)* Do you have some dolls

at your house?

Sarah: Oh, yes. I have a lot of dolls.

Mr. Fred: I know a little girl whose name is Melinda. She doesn't have a doll. Don't you think it would make her happy if you gave her one of yours?

Sarah *(thoughtfully)*: I suppose.

Mr. Fred: And that would be like giving to Jesus because he taught us to share.

Sarah: Okay. I'll do it.

Mr. Fred: Let me know when you choose the doll to give away. I'll get Melinda to wait here with me.

Sarah: Thank you. See you, Mr. Fred. *(Exits.)*

Gary *(enters)*: Mr. Fred, I was hoping I'd find you out here.

Mr. Fred: Hey, Gary. What you up to?

Gary: I was just trying to figure out something. Maybe you can help me. I want to do something special for Jesus at this Christmastime and I don't know what to do.

Mr. Fred: Gary, I think you are just the one to help Mrs. Knight with her Christmas shopping. You know she can't walk around easily the way we do, but if you would just push her in her wheelchair, she could look around the store and choose the things she wants to buy.

Gary: But is that doing something for Jesus?

Mr. Fred: Of course it is. Jesus said when people do good things for others, it's just the same as doing it for Him.

Gary: I'll go see Mrs. Knight right now so we can make plans. Thank you, Mr. Fred. *(Exits.)*

Tamra *(enters)*: Mr. Fred, do you have time to help me?

Mr. Fred: Sure I do, child. What do you need?

Tamra: Our Sunday school teacher said we should do something special for Jesus at Christmastime because it's His birthday, but I don't know what to do.

Mr. Fred: Tamra, you know Jesus is in Heaven, but if you will do something for somebody who really needs something special, it will be like doing it for Jesus.

Tamra: But I don't know anybody who needs something special.

Mr. Fred *(points to side of stage)*: You see that house down at the corner? Yesterday I met the couple that moved in there. They are new in town and don't have friends here yet. In fact, they are older people and I expect they are a little bit lonely.

Tamra: But what can I do?

Mr. Fred: How about helping your mom make some cookies and taking some to their house? I'm sure they would enjoy a visit from you, too.

Tamra: That's it! We'll make cookies! Thanks, Mr. Fred. *(Exits.)*

Sidney *(enters)*: Hey, Mr. Fred.

Mr. Fred: Hi, Sidney.

Sidney: I have a problem.

Mr. Fred: What is it, Sidney?

Sidney: I'm trying to think of something special to do for Christmas. You know, like I am doing it for Jesus.

Mr. Fred: And you can't think of what to do?

Sidney: Maybe you can help me.

Mr. Fred: I do know a boy who is very poor. He snagged his one good pair of jeans yesterday while he was climbing a tree, and he is about your size.

Sidney: I have plenty of jeans. Do you think he'd like to have a pair of mine?

Mr. Fred: I'm sure it would make him very happy. And his mother, too.

Sidney: Thanks, Mr. Fred. I'll check with Mother right now. *(Exits.)*

Ashley *(enters with Sam)*: Mr. Fred, what are you making?

Mr. Fred: Well, I think it's going to be a surprise.

Sam: We were just talking about Christmas. You know it's Jesus' birthday?

Mr. Fred: Yes, I know.

Sam: We need to think of something special for Jesus, don't we?

Mr. Fred: Sounds like a good idea to me.

Ashley: We can't think what to do.

Mr. Fred: Didn't I hear you talking about that family across town whose house burned?

Sam: That's right. Charles is on my ball team.

Mr. Fred: I hear there's a drive to get them some clothes and things to help them out. Maybe you have something you'd like to give.

Sam: I have a new jacket I got for my birthday. It's pretty cool, but I already have another one. I could give Charles my new jacket.

Ashley: What about me? Nobody in that family is my size.

Mr. Fred: Maybe there is something else you could share.

Ashley: Like what? What can a fellow share? Oh, I know! I can give some of my allowance. I heard my mom say she is collecting from people in our neighborhood to help the family that got burned out.

Mr. Fred: Sounds like you have it all worked out. *(Boys exit.)*

Mr. Fred *(to himself):* I sure am glad to see children thinking about something other than themselves during Christmastime. When I was at the store the other night, I just stood there watching all those kids talking to that store Santa Claus. All I heard them say was, "I want. I want. I want." Now when I see children like these I've been talking to, who are really interested in doing something for somebody else, it just warms my heart.

Little Stephanie *(enters)*: Hey, Mr. Fred.

Mr. Fred *(stops whittling)*: Now here is my little friend, Stephanie. Come on over and talk to me. *(She sits on his knee.)* What's on your mind today, child?

Little Stephanie: I want to do something to make Jesus know I love Him.

Mr. Fred: That sounds good to me. What do you want to do?

Little Stephanie: I don't know. I can't give him a hug 'cause he's in Heaven.

Mr. Fred: That's right, He is.

Little Stephanie: And I can't make Him a Christmas card like I do for my mom 'cause I can't give it to Him.

Mr. Fred: You've really been thinking about this, haven't you Stephanie?

Little Stephanie: Yes, but I still don't know what to do.

Mr. Fred: I know something you can do. Sing Him a song.

Little Stephanie: Will Jesus hear me sing?

Mr. Fred: I'm sure He will. You can talk it over with your mom. Maybe you can sing it at church. You remember how good it made you feel when your mom sang you a lullaby at night when you were a baby? It made you know she loved you special.

Little Stephanie: My mom still sings to me sometimes.

Mr. Fred: And it makes you feel good?

Little Stephanie: Oh, yes. My mom sings at church you know. But sometimes she just sings special for me.

Mr. Fred: Then you can sing for Jesus.

Little Stephanie: And Mr. Fred, when I learn my song to sing, I'll come back and tell you.

Mr. Fred: Good girl, Stephanie.

Little Stephanie: See you later, Mr. Fred. *(Exits.)*

Katrina *(enters holding her mother's hand)*: Mr. Fred, Mom's taking me with her to see Mrs. Thorpe.

Katrina's Mother: How are you today, Mr. Fred?

Mr. Fred: Fine thank you. *(Speaking to Katrina.)* And what is this you are doing today, Katrina?

Katrina: We're going to see Mrs. Thorpe. She hasn't got a little girl or a little granddaughter. Mom says if we go and visit her, then I can decide what kind of Christmas card to make for her. I want to know what her favorite color is.

Mr. Fred: Well, you have a good visit now. Let me know about that special Christmas card you're going to make. *(Katrina and Mom exit.)* Sometimes I get to thinking about the condition the world is in, and I wonder what is going to happen to all of us. Then I have a good day like this, and I see there is still a whole lot of good in the world.

Children still know how to love one another. Mothers are still training children to think of other people, and it all makes sense again. Christmas means love with a capital "L."

Scene 2

Same place Christmas Eve—Mr. Fred is whittling and humming or singing a Christmas carol.

Sarah *(enters)*: Hey, Mr. Fred. I got it. I got the doll. *(Hands it to Mr. Fred.)*

Mr. Fred: This is a beautiful doll, Sarah.

Sarah: I know. *(Takes doll back—hugs her.)* I really love her, but if that little girl doesn't have a doll, I'm sure she will love her, too.

Mr. Fred: That she will.

Sarah: Maybe we can let our dolls visit each other sometimes. Where is she, Mr. Fred? You said she would wait here with you. And what is her name again?

Mr. Fred: Melinda. She said she would come over here about—*(As Melinda enters.)* Here she is now. Hey, Melinda come on over and see Sarah.

Sarah: I brought you one of my dolls, Melinda. *(Hands doll over.)*

Melinda *(examines doll)*: Oh, she is beautiful. What is her name?

Sarah: Well,—I—maybe you want to give her a name. She's your doll now.

Melinda: Thanks Sarah. *(Hugs doll.)* I always wanted a doll I could name Amy. *(Two girls go aside and talk quietly.)*

Sidney *(enters)*: Mr. Fred, I have a pair of jeans for that boy you told me about. But you didn't tell me where he lives.

Mr. Fred: Well, Sidney, he is coming by to see me today. Maybe if you just wait around, he'll be here soon.

Sidney: You still working on that same piece of wood, Mr. Fred?

Mr. Fred: No, I finished that whistle. I'm starting another one now.

Boy *(enters)*: Mr. Fred?

Mr. Fred: Oh, here is my friend now. How you doing today?

Boy: Okay. I guess.

Mr. Fred: I have another friend here who has something he wants to give you.

Sidney *(hands over jeans)*: Mr. Fred told me you snagged your jeans, and I have this extra pair. You reckon you can wear these?

Boy: Sure. They'll be just right. Thanks.

Sidney: Where is that tree you were climbing? I like to climb trees, too.

(Boys leave while talking to each other.)

Katrina *(enters with Mom)*: Hey, Mr. Fred. I want you to see the Christmas card I made. Mrs. Thorpe's favorite color is pink, so I put some pink flowers right here. See. *(Hands it to Mr. Fred.)* She said she likes Christmas colors, too, so of course there is some red and green to make it look like Christmas.

Mr. Fred *(reads from inside card)*: "For a special lady. Merry Christmas." *(To Katrina.)* You did a good job, Katrina. I know Mrs. Thorpe will just love this. *(Katrina and Mom exit.)*

Tamra *(enters with plate of cookies)*: Mr. Fred, I'm on my way to the house at the end of the block. We made chocolate chip cookies. Boy are they good! I want you to have one, too.

Mr. Fred *(takes cookie and bites it)*: Mmmm good. I know the new couple will like these.

Tamra: See you, Mr. Fred. *(Exits.)*

Sam *(enters with Ashley)*: Hey, Mr. Fred, we're back.

Mr. Fred: Good to see you. You know I always like for you to stop by to talk with me.

Sam: Here's that jacket I was telling you about. *(Shows it.)*

Mr. Fred: That is a good jacket, Sam. Is that the new one you got for your birthday? Did you talk to your mom about giving it away?

Sam: Sure. Mom said it was a good idea. Especially since I like the old one better anyway.

Mr. Fred: I guess that makes sense.

Ashley: I have ten quarters from my money bank to give. And Mom said I could help her collect on this block. She gave me this box to put the money in.

Mr. Fred *(takes bill from pocket)*: Let me contribute something, too. You're doing a good thing, Ashley. You are not only sharing your money but your time as well. *(Sees Charles as he enters.)* Look, here comes Charles now.

Sam: Hey, Charles. I was going to look for you.

Charles: Hey, Sam.

Mr. Fred: Sam has something special for you, Charles.

Sam: Yeah, I thought you would like to have this jacket since you lost everything in the fire.

Charles *(puts on jacket)*: That's cool. Thanks, Sam.

Ashley: We're getting some money together for the whole family, Charles. I've already put some of my allowance in the box. Mom says we will have it all together in a little while. See you later. *(Exits.)*

Sam: Tell me about it, Charles. Where were you when that fire started? *(They walk to side of stage talking.)*

Mr. Fred: I think this is going to be my best Christmas. The happy faces are brighter than the lights on the tree. It's just wonderful.

Gary *(enters pushing Mrs. Knight in chair)*: We just finished our shopping, Mr. Fred.

Mrs. Knight: We had a wonderful time. This young man was just a godsend to me.

Mr. Fred: I'm glad you stopped to see me. Looks like you had a good day.

Gary: Mrs. Knight had a long list, but I think she got everything.

Mrs. Knight: It has been so long since I've been on a shopping spree, I just didn't know when to stop. Now when I get all these presents wrapped, I'll be able to make some people happy, too.

Little Stephanie *(enters)*: Mr. Fred, I'm ready with my song for Jesus.

Mr. Fred: Oh, good! And this is a perfect time for you to practice singing it. I know Mrs. Knight would enjoy hearing you sing.

Little Stephanie: Okay. *(Moves aside, holding mike.)* Mom says I'll use a mike at church so I've been practicing with this one. *(Sings "Away in a Manger.")*

Mrs. Knight *(applauds)*: Oh, that was so sweet. Just let me give you a great big hug, Stephanie.

Mr. Fred: I know Jesus will like that song, Stephanie. It will be a happy birthday song for Him.

Stephanie: I gotta go. See you. *(Exits.)*

Mr. Fred: This must be a happy Christmas for many people. *(Calls out in loud voice.)* Hey, you guys wherever you are! Come on back and let's sing a song together. *(Cast assembles as Mr. Fred speaks.)*

Mr. Fred: When people all over the world learn to share like these folks are doing tonight, we will have learned what real love is all about. The Christmas season always reminds me of the words of Jesus. When He was a grown man, teaching the people the way of the Lord and emphasizing the necessity of helping those in need He said, " . . . Whatever you did for one of the least of these brothers of mine, you did for me" (Matthew 25:40 New International Version).

Tonight our hearts are full of love and joy of the Christmas season. I'll just ask all of you to stand and sing with those of us on stage "Joy to the World, the Lord is Come!" *(Cast members join hands as they sing.)*

All sing, then program leader leads in prayer.